Look and See

Susannah Reed

NATIONAL GEOGRAPHIC
LEARNING

Australia • Brazil • Mexico • Singapore • United Kingdom • United States

Scope and Sequence

What's your name? p. 4 — *What's your name?* *My name's …*

		Words	Structure	Value	Letters and Sounds/ Numbers	Content Connections: Video	Content Connections: Project
1 Hello! p. 5		*Hello!* *Goodbye.* *Say hello.* *Wave goodbye.* *Stand up.* *Sit down.* *Open your book.* *Close your book.*	*How are you?* *I'm fine, thank you.*	Make friends.	Aa /æ/	Social Science How do people say hello around the world?	A puppet
2 School p. 11		*school* *apron* *bag* *chair* *crayon* *pencil* *table*	*What's this?* *It's a pencil.*	Take care of your things.	1, 2	Social Science How are classrooms different around the world?	A pencil holder
3 Colors p. 17		*paint* *blue* *green* *orange* *purple* *red* *yellow*	*What color is the book?* *It's red.*	Be creative.	Ee /ɛ/	Art What happens when we mix primary colors?	A squish painting
4 Toys p. 23		*train* *ball* *bus* *car* *doll* *puppet* *teddy bear*	*I have a ball.*	Share your toys.	3, 4	Social Science What land transportation do we use?	A bus collage
5 Let's Move! p. 29		*body* *arms* *feet* *hands* *head* *legs* *tummy*	*Touch your head.* *Move your hands.*	Be active.	Ii /ɪ/	Music, Physical Education What are different ways to dance?	A shaker

		Words	Structure	Value	Letters and Sounds/ Numbers	Content Connections: Video	Content Connections: Project
6 **Food**		*apple, banana, carrot, cracker, milk, orange, water*	*I like oranges.* *Me, too!*	Choose healthy food.	5, 6	Science How do plants grow?	An apple tree book
7 **My Family**		*photo, brother, dad, grandma, grandpa, mom, sister*	*This is my mom.*	Be good to your family.	Oo /ɑ/	Science Do animals live in families?	A photo frame
8 **On the Farm**		*chicken, cat, cow, dog, goat, horse, sheep*	*Is it a cow? No, it isn't.* *Is it a horse? Yes, it is.*	Take care of animals.	7, 8	Science What do we get from farm animals?	A paper-plate sheep
9 **My Clothes**		*hat, jacket, shoes, shorts, socks, T-shirt, black, brown, white*	*My T-shirt is orange.* *My shorts are red.*	Dress yourself.	Uu /ʌ/	Social Science How is wool made into clothes?	A yarn sweater
10 **Outside**		*frog, bird, fish, flower, leaf, rainbow, tree*	*How many birds?* *Four birds.*	Explore outside.	9, 10	Science What animals use camouflage?	A camouflaged animal picture

Girls shaking hands at school, Bangladesh

STRUCTURE: *What's your name? My name's Jian.*

1 Look and see. **2** TR: 0.1 Listen and say. **3** TR: 0.2 Listen and sing. **4** TR: 0.3 Sing and do.

UNIT 1

Hello!

Happy children at school, Mongolia

LESSON 1

NEW WORDS: *Hello!, Goodbye.*

1 Look and see. **2** SC: 1 Watch. **3** TR: 1.1 Listen and say. **4** TR: 1.2 Listen and do.

LESSON 2

NEW WORDS: *Say hello. Wave goodbye. Stand up. Sit down. Open your book. Close your book.*

1 TR: 1.3 Listen and point. **2** TR: 1.4 Listen and do. **3** TR: 1.5 Listen again and do.

LESSON 3

STRUCTURE: *How are you? I'm fine, thank you.*

1 TR: 1.6 Listen and point. **2** TR: 1.7 Listen and say. **3** Play and say.

Friends playing together, Malaysia

VALUE

Make friends.

LESSON 4

SONG AND VALUE: *Make friends.*

1 TR: 1.8 Listen and point. **2** TR: 1.9 Listen and sing. **3** TR: 1.10 Sing and do. **4** Stick.

Aa

A a

Aa

LESSON 5

LETTERS AND SOUNDS: Aa, /æ/

1 TR: 1.11 Listen and point. **2** TR: 1.12 Listen. Trace and say. **3** TR: 1.13 Listen and chant. **4** Draw and say.

Inupiaq children saying hello, Alaska, USA

LESSON 6

VIDEO **Content Word:** *world*

1 Look and see. **2** SC: 2 Watch. **3** SC: 2 Watch and say.

LESSON 7

PROJECT

1 Make.

UNIT 2
School

A girl on her way to school, Ivory Coast

LESSON 1

NEW WORD: *school*

1 Look and see. **2** SC: 3 Watch. **3** TR: 2.1 Listen and say. **4** TR: 2.2 Listen and do.

Boy at school, Guatemala

LESSON 2

NEW WORDS: *apron, bag, chair, crayon, pencil, table*

1 TR: 2.3 Listen and point. **2** TR: 2.4 Listen and say. **3** TR: 2.5 Listen and chant.

LESSON 3

STRUCTURE: *What's this? It's a pencil.*

1 TR: 2.6 Listen and point. **2** TR: 2.7 Listen and say. **3** Play and say.

Boys reading together, UAE

VALUE

Take care of your things.

LESSON 4

SONG AND VALUE: *Take care of your things.*

1 TR: 2.8 Listen and point. **2** TR: 2.9 Listen and sing. **3** TR: 2.10 Sing and do. **4** Stick.

LESSON 5

NUMBERS: 1, 2

1 TR: 2.11 Listen and point. **2** TR: 2.12 Listen. Trace and say. **3** TR: 2.13 Listen and chant. **4** Draw and count.

LESSON 6

VIDEO **Content Words:** *classroom, different, fun, teacher*

1 Look and see. **2** SC: 4 Watch. **3** SC: 4 Watch and say.

LESSON 7

PROJECT

1 Make.

UNIT 3 Colors

A girl covered in paint

LESSON 1

NEW WORD: *paint*

1 Look and see. **2** SC: 5 Watch. **3** TR: 3.1 Listen and say. **4** TR: 3.2 Listen and do.

red | orange | yellow | green | blue | purple

LESSON 2

NEW WORDS: *blue, green, orange, purple, red, yellow*

1 TR: 3.3 Listen and point. **2** TR: 3.4 Listen and say. **3** TR: 3.5 Listen and chant.

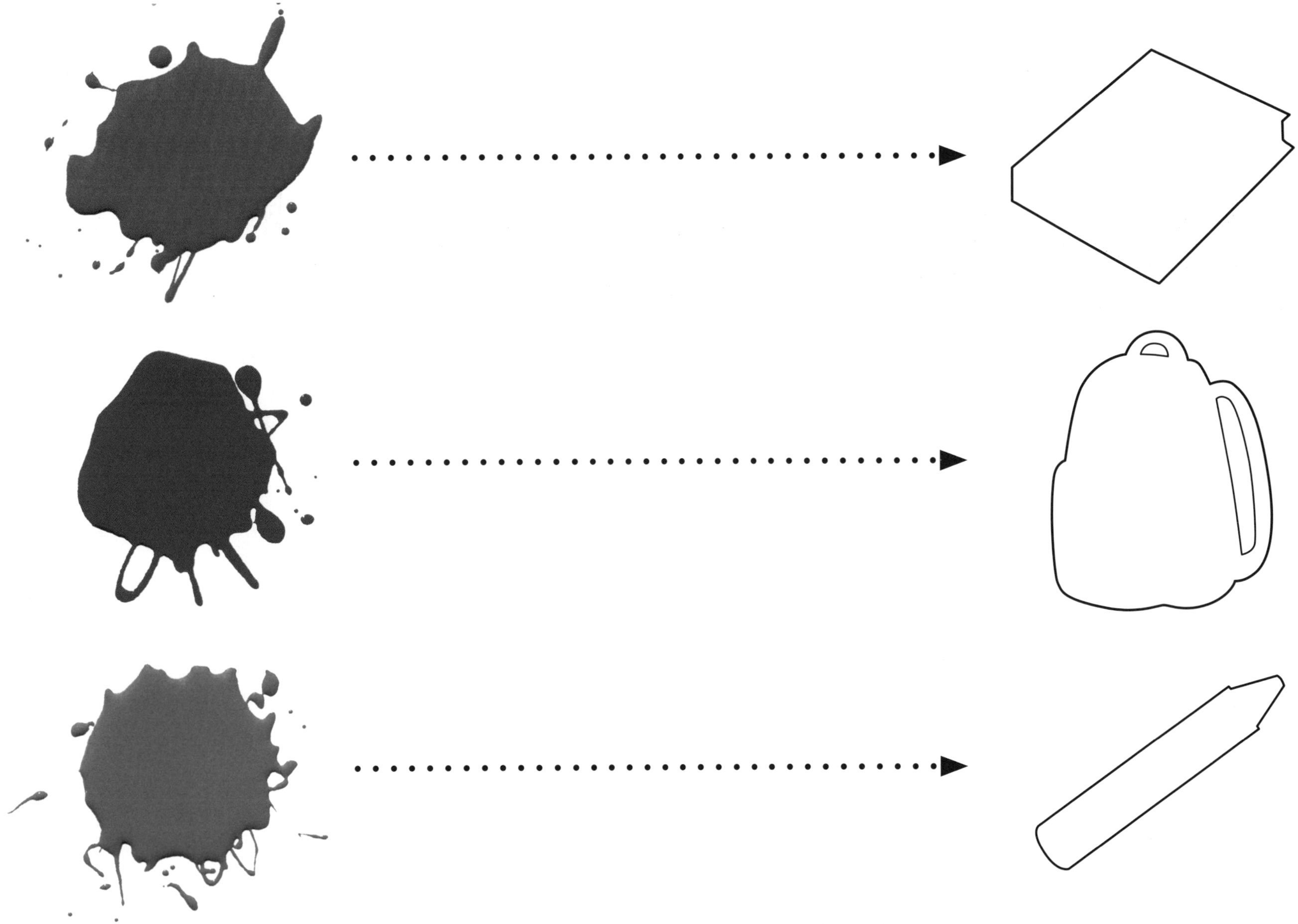

LESSON 3

STRUCTURE: *What color is the book? It's red.*

1 TR: 3.6 Listen and point. Draw. **2** TR: 3.7 Listen and say. **3** Color and say.

A child with artwork, Brazil

VALUE

Be creative.

LESSON 4

SONG AND VALUE: *Be creative.*

1 TR: 3.8 Listen and point. **2** TR: 3.9 Listen and sing. **3** TR: 3.10 Sing and do. **4** Stick.

E → e

Ee → 

LETTERS AND SOUNDS: Ee, /ɛ/

1 TR: 3.11 Listen and point. **2** TR: 3.12 Listen. Trace and say. **3** TR: 3.13 Listen and chant. **4** Draw and say.

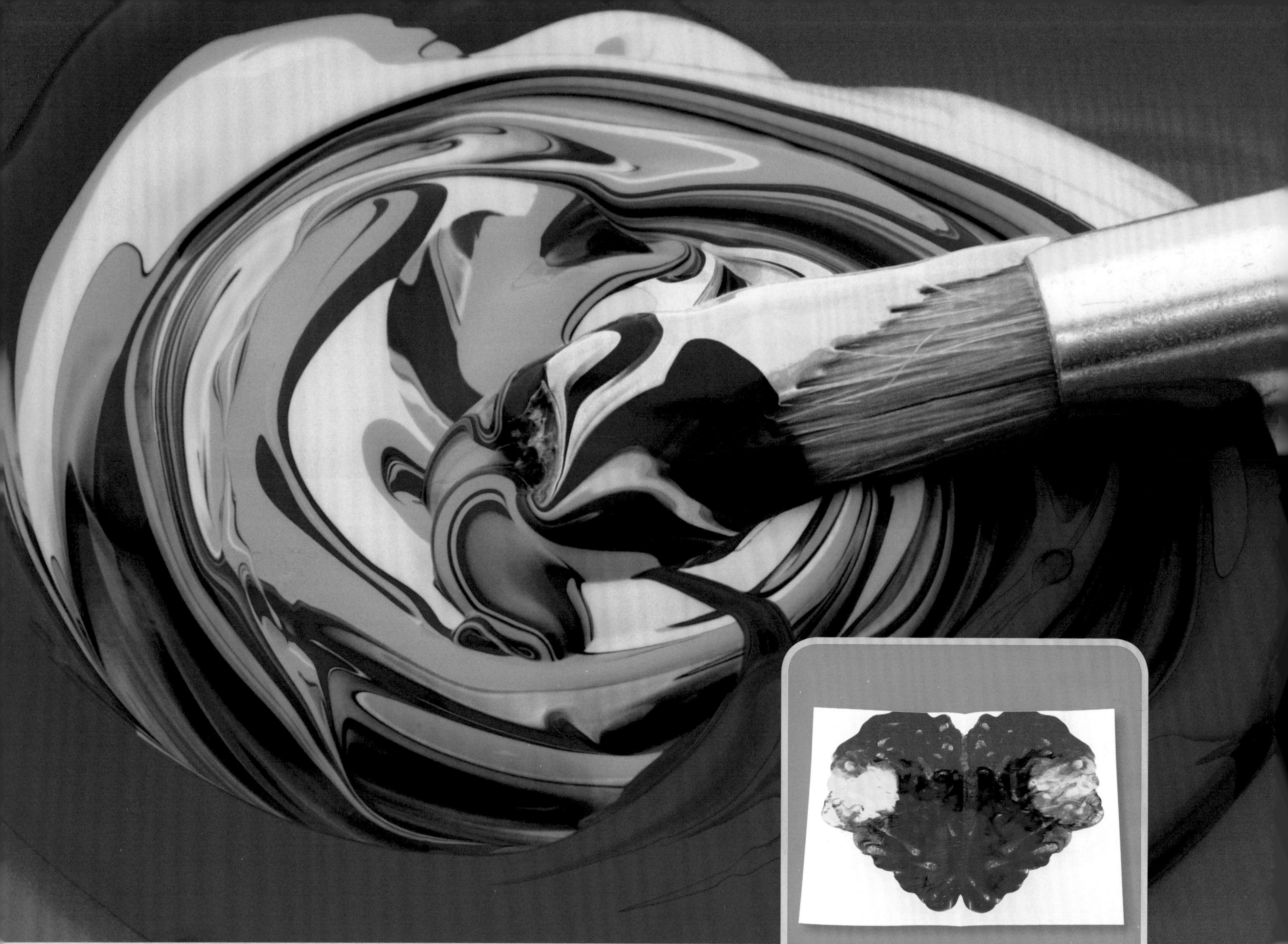

LESSON 6

VIDEO **Content Words:** *make, picture*

1 Look and see. **2** SC: 6 Watch. **3** SC: 6 Watch and say.

LESSON 7

PROJECT

1 Make.

UNIT 4 Toys

A train show at the New York Botanical Garden, USA

LESSON 1

NEW WORD: *train*

1 Look and see. **2** SC: 7 Watch. **3** TR: 4.1 Listen and say. **4** TR: 4.2 Listen and do.

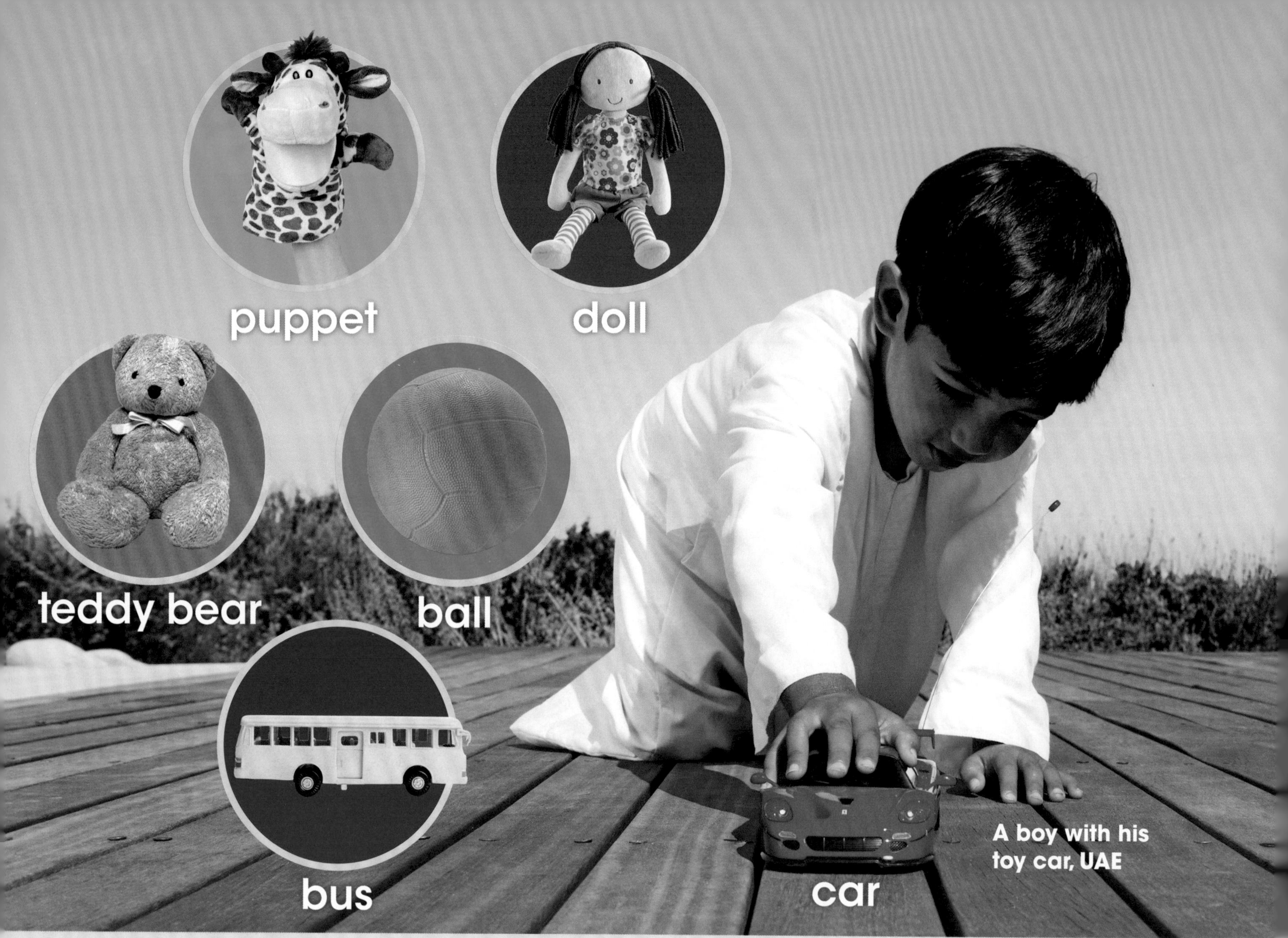

A boy with his toy car, UAE

LESSON 2

NEW WORDS: *ball, bus, car, doll, puppet, teddy bear*

1 TR: 4.3 Listen and point. **2** TR: 4.4 Listen and say. **3** TR: 4.5 Listen and chant.

LESSON 3

STRUCTURE: *I have a ball.*

1 TR: 4.6 Listen and point. **2** TR: 4.7 Listen and say. **3** Play and say.

VALUE

Share your toys.

LESSON 4

SONG AND VALUE: *Share your toys.*

1 TR: 4.8 Listen and point. **2** TR: 4.9 Listen and sing. **3** TR: 4.10 Sing and do. **4** Stick.

LESSON 5

NUMBERS: 3, 4

1 TR: 4.11 Listen and point. **2** TR: 4.12 Listen. Trace and say. **3** TR: 4.13 Listen and chant. **4** Draw and count.

Trains, buses, and cars, Malaysia

LESSON 6

VIDEO **Content Words:** *big, pink, small*

1 Look and see. **2** SC: 8 Watch. **3** SC: 8 Watch, point, and say.

LESSON 7

PROJECT

1 Make.

UNIT 5

Let's Move!

A boy practicing kung fu, China

LESSON 1

NEW WORD: *body*

1 Look and see. **2** SC: 9 Watch. **3** TR: 5.1 Listen and say. **4** TR: 5.2 Listen and do.

LESSON 2

NEW WORDS: *arms, feet, hands, head, legs, tummy*

1 TR: 5.3 Listen and point. **2** TR: 5.4 Listen and say. **3** TR: 5.5 Listen and chant.

touch

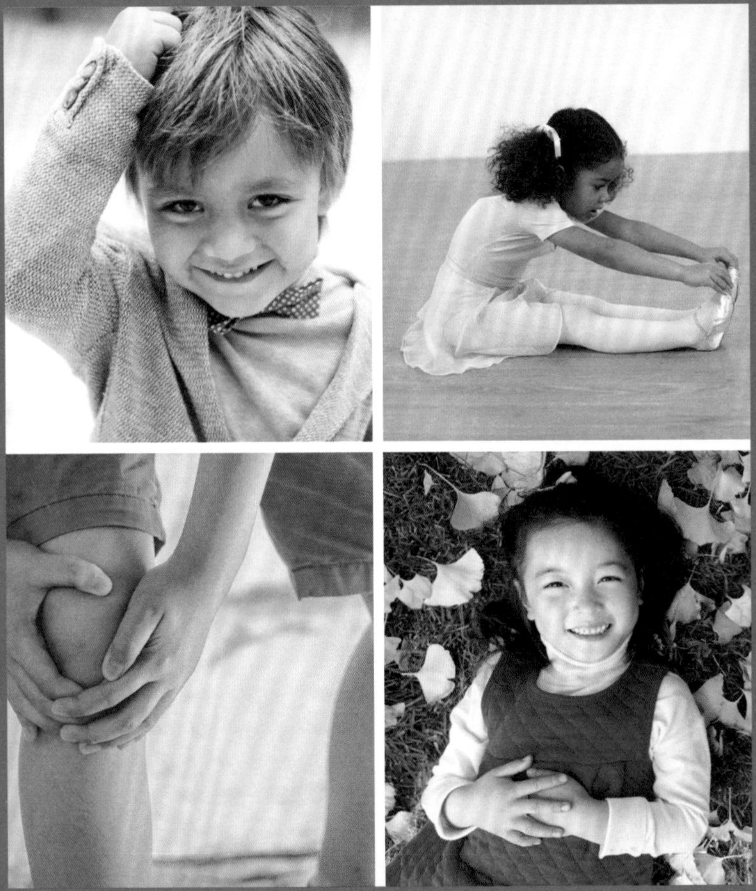

move

LESSON 3

STRUCTURE: *Touch your head. Move your hands.*

1 TR: 5.6 Listen and point. **2** TR: 5.7 Listen and say. **3** Play and say.

Children dancing together, China

VALUE

Be active.

LESSON 4

SONG AND VALUE: *Be active.*

1 Look and see. **2** TR: 5.8 Listen and do. **3** TR: 5.9 Listen and sing. **4** Stick.

I → i

Ii → 

LESSON 5

LETTERS AND SOUNDS: Ii, /ɪ/

1 TR: 5.10 Listen and point. **2** TR: 5.11 Listen. Trace and say. **3** TR: 5.12 Listen and chant. **4** Draw and say.

Dancers at a festival, Mexico

LESSON 6

VIDEO **Content Words:** *clap, dance, left, right, stomp*

1 Look and see. **2** SC: 10 Watch. **3** SC: 10 Watch and do.

LESSON 7

PROJECT

1 Make.

UNIT 6 Food

An apple orchard, USA

LESSON 1

NEW WORD: *apple*

1 Look and see. **2** SC: 11 Watch. **3** TR: 6.1 Listen and say. **4** TR: 6.2 Listen and do.

LESSON 2

NEW WORDS: *banana, carrot, cracker, milk, orange, water*

1 TR: 6.3 Listen and point. **2** TR: 6.4 Listen and say. **3** TR: 6.5 Listen and chant.

LESSON 3

STRUCTURE: *I like oranges. Me, too!*

1 TR: 6.6 Listen and point. **2** TR: 6.7 Listen and say. **3** Color and say.

A fruit market, Indonesia

LESSON 4

SONG AND VALUE: *Choose healthy food.*

1 TR: 6.8 Listen and point. **2** TR: 6.9 Listen and sing. **3** TR: 6.10 Sing and do. **4** Stick.

VALUE

Choose healthy food.

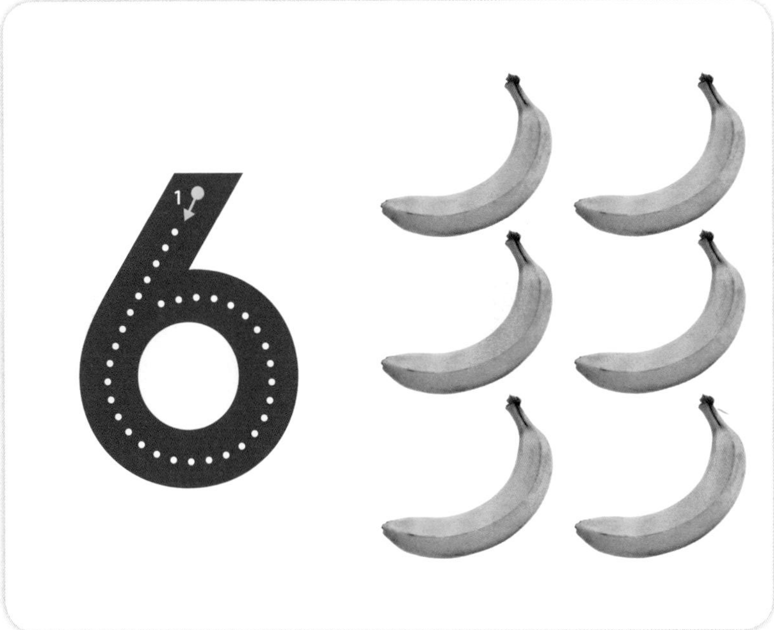

LESSON 5

NUMBERS: 5, 6

1 TR: 6.11 Listen and point. **2** TR: 6.12 Listen. Trace and say. **3** TR: 6.13 Listen and chant. **4** Draw and count.

LESSON 6

VIDEO **Content Words:** *grow, plant, seed, tree*

1 Look and see. **2** SC: 12 Watch. **3** SC: 12 Watch, point, and say.

LESSON 7

PROJECT

1 Make.

UNIT

My Family 7

A family celebration, China

LESSON 1

NEW WORD: *photo*

1 Look and see. **2** SC: 13 Watch. **3** TR: 7.1 Listen and say. **4** TR: 7.2 Listen and do.

LESSON 2

NEW WORDS: *brother, dad, grandma, grandpa, mom, sister*

1 TR: 7.3 Listen and point. **2** TR: 7.4 Listen and say. **3** TR: 7.5 Listen and chant.

LESSON 3

STRUCTURE: *This is my mom.*

1 TR: 7.6 Listen and point. **2** TR: 7.7 Listen and say. **3** Draw and say.

A boy and his grandma, Slovakia

VALUE

Be good to your family.

LESSON 4

SONG AND VALUE: *Be good to your family.*

1 TR: 7.8 Listen and point. **2** TR: 7.9 Listen and sing. **3** TR: 7.10 Sing and do. **4** Stick.

Oo

O o

Oo

LESSON 5

LETTERS AND SOUNDS: Oo, /ɑ/

1 TR: 7.11 Listen and point. **2** TR: 7.12 Listen. Trace and say. **3** TR: 7.13 Listen and chant. **4** Draw and say.

Lions and elephants, Kenya

LESSON 6

VIDEO **Content Words:** *baby, cub, lion*

1 Look and see. **2** SC: 14 Watch. **3** SC: 14 Watch, point, and say.

LESSON 7

PROJECT

1 Make.

UNIT 8

On the Farm

Chickens leaving their coop, USA

LESSON 1

NEW WORD: *chicken*

1 Look and see. **2** SC: 15 Watch. **3** TR: 8.1 Listen and say. **4** TR: 8.2 Listen and do.

LESSON 2

NEW WORDS: *cat, cow, dog, goat, horse, sheep*

1 TR: 8.3 Listen and point. **2** TR: 8.4 Listen and say. **3** TR: 8.5 Listen and chant.

LESSON 3

STRUCTURE: *Is it a cow? No, it isn't. Is it a horse? Yes, it is.*

1 TR: 8.6 Listen and point. **2** TR: 8.7 Listen and say. **3** Play and say.

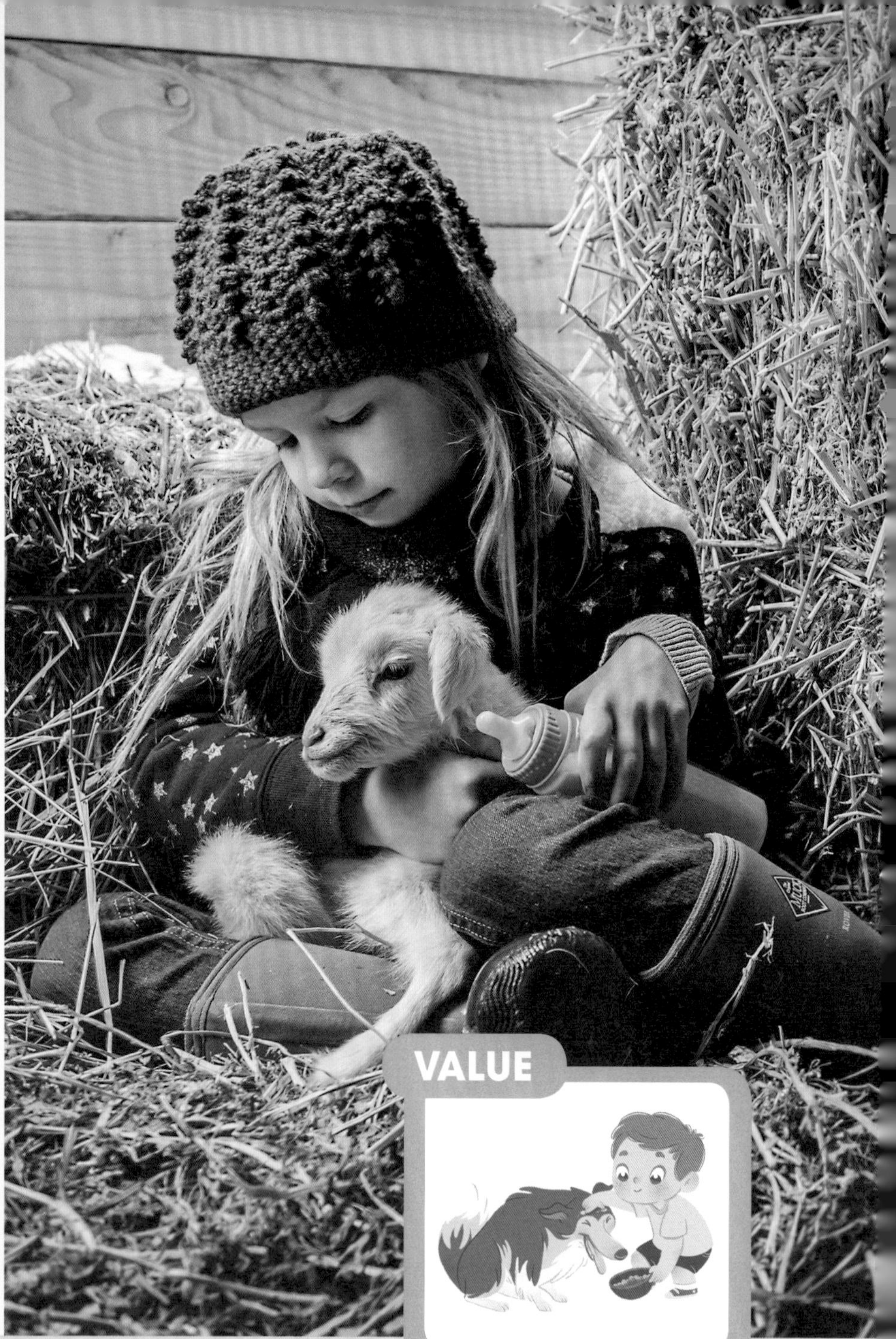

VALUE

Take care of animals.

LESSON 4

SONG AND VALUE: *Take care of animals.*

1 TR: 8.8 Listen and point. **2** TR: 8.9 Listen and sing. **3** TR: 8.10 Sing and do. **4** Stick.

7

8

LESSON 5

NUMBERS: 7, 8

1 TR: 8.11 Listen and point. **2** TR: 8.12 Listen. Trace and say. **3** TR: 8.13 Listen and chant. **4** Draw and count.

LESSON 6

VIDEO **Content Words:** *egg, wool*

1 Look and see. **2** SC: 16 Watch. **3** SC: 16 Watch, point, and say.

LESSON 7

PROJECT

1 Make.

UNIT

My Clothes 9

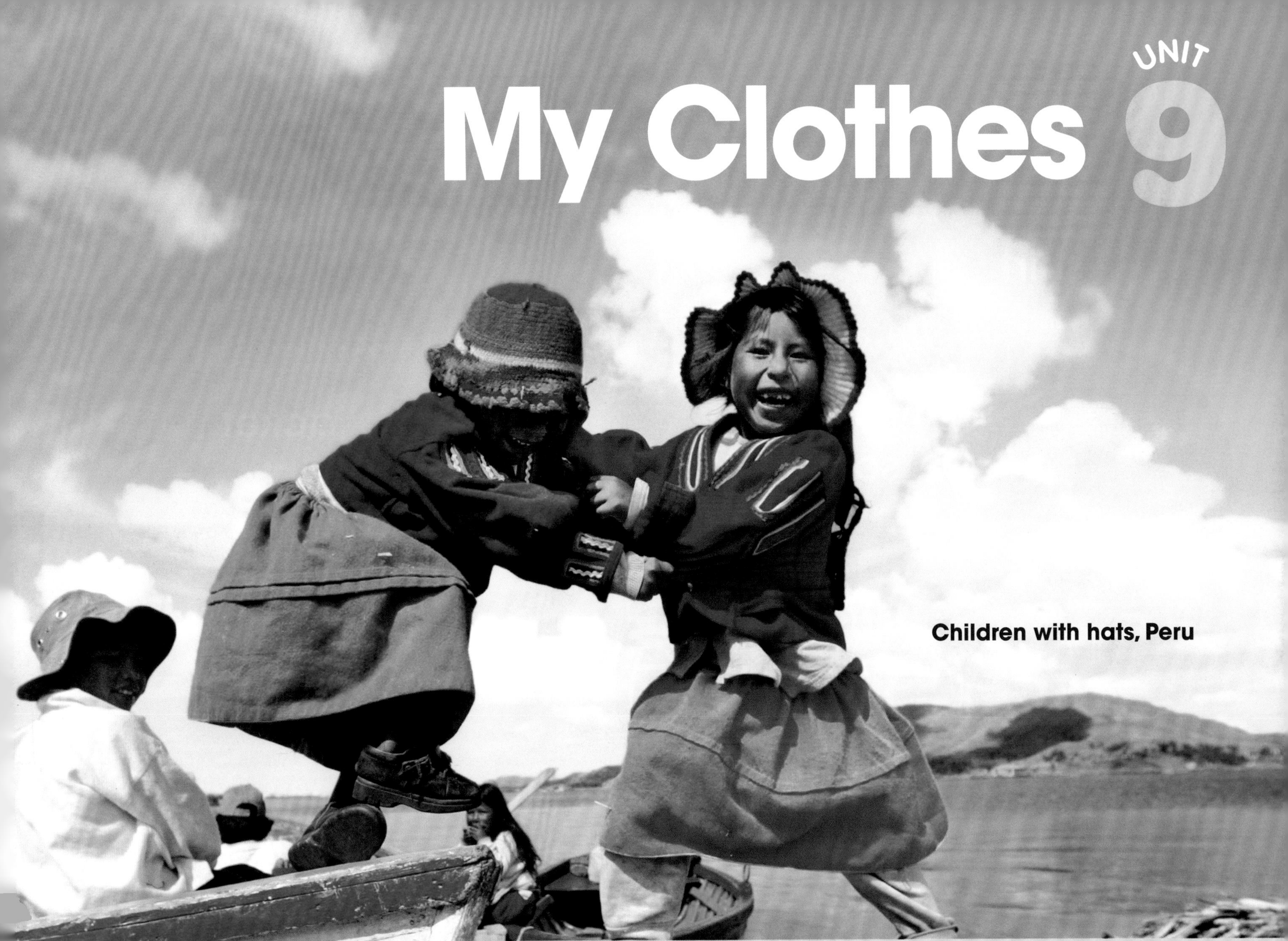

Children with hats, Peru

LESSON 1

NEW WORD: *hat*

1 Look and see. **2** SC: 17 Watch. **3** TR: 9.1 Listen and say. **4** TR: 9.2 Listen and do.

Girls at an ice festival, South Korea

LESSON 2

NEW WORDS: *jacket, shoes, shorts, socks, T-shirt; black, brown, white*

1 TR: 9.3 Listen and point. **2** TR: 9.4 Listen and say. **3** TR: 9.5 Listen and chant.

LESSON 3

STRUCTURE: *My T-shirt is orange. My shorts are red.*

1 TR: 9.6 Listen and point. **2** TR: 9.7 Listen and say. **3** Play and say.

VALUE

Dress yourself.

LESSON 4

SONG AND VALUE: *Dress yourself.*

1 TR: 9.8 Listen and point. **2** TR: 9.9 Listen and sing. **3** TR: 9.10 Sing and do. **4** Stick.

Uu

U u

Uu

LESSON 5

LETTERS AND SOUNDS: Uu, /ʌ/

1 TR: 9.11 Listen and point. **2** TR: 9.12 Listen. Trace and say. **3** TR: 9.13 Listen and chant. **4** Draw and say.

LESSON 6

VIDEO **Content Words:** *scarf, sweater, yarn*

1 Look and see. **2** SC: 18 Watch. **3** SC: 18 Watch, point, and say.

LESSON 7

PROJECT

1 Make.

LESSON 1

NEW WORD: *frog*

1 Look and see. **2** SC: 19 Watch. **3** TR: 10.1 Listen and say. **4** TR: 10.2 Listen and do.

The Alps, Italy

LESSON 2

NEW WORDS: *bird, fish, flower, leaf, rainbow, tree*

1 TR: 10.3 Listen and point. **2** TR: 10.4 Listen and say. **3** TR: 10.5 Listen and chant.

LESSON 3

STRUCTURE: *How many birds? Four birds.*

1 TR: 10.6 Listen and point. **2** TR: 10.7 Listen and say. **3** Play and say.

Three parrots, Costa Rica

VALUE

Explore outside.

LESSON 4

SONG AND VALUE: *Explore outside.*

1 TR: 10.8 Listen and point. **2** TR: 10.9 Listen and sing. **3** TR: 10.10 Sing and do. **4** Stick.

9

10

LESSON 5

NUMBERS: 9, 10

1 TR: 10.11 Listen and point. **2** TR: 10.12 Listen. Trace and say. **3** TR: 10.13 Listen and chant. **4** Draw and count.

LESSON 6

VIDEO **Content Words:** *bug, lizard*

1 Look and see. **2** SC: 20 Watch. **3** SC: 20 Watch, point, and say.

LESSON 7

PROJECT

1 Make.

UNIT 1

Hello!

Hello, my friend.
How are you?
I'm fine, thank you.
I'm fine, too.

[Chorus]
Let's say hello!
Let's make friends.
Let's make friends together.

Hello, my friend.
How are you?
I'm fine, thank you.
I'm fine, too.

[Chorus]

UNIT 2

School

What's this?
It's a book.
It's my book.
My nice, new book!

Take care of your book.
Take care of your things.

What's this?
It's a pencil.
It's my pencil.
My nice, new pencil!

Take care of your pencil.
Take care of your things.

UNIT 3

Colors

Here is red and yellow, too.
Here is green and blue.

[Chorus]
Look at the colors,
beautiful colors!
What colors can you see?

Here is green and yellow, too.
Here is red and blue.

[Chorus]

UNIT 4

Toys

I have a car.
And I have a car.
Two cars—one and two.
One for me and one for you.

Let's share the cars.
Let's share the toys!

I have a ball.
And I have a ball.
Two balls—one and two.
One for me and one for you.

Let's share the balls.
Let's share the toys!

UNIT
5

Let's Move!

Move your arms.
Move your hands.
Up and down,
arms and hands.

[Chorus]
Let's be active:
one, two, three!
Move your body.
Move with me!

Touch your legs.
Touch your feet.
Hands down,
and touch your feet.

[Chorus]

UNIT
6

Food

I like apples.
I like oranges.
I like bananas, too.

[Chorus]
Look at the food.
It's healthy food.
Food for me and you.

I like bananas.
I like apples.
I like oranges, too.

[Chorus]

UNIT 8

On the Farm

What's this? Is it a horse?
Yes, it is. It's a horse.
It's my horse, Maxi.
Here you are, Maxi.
This is for you.

Take care of your horse.
Take care of animals.

What's this? Is it a goat?
No, it isn't. It's a lamb.
It's my lamb, Suzy.
Here you are, Suzy.
This is for you.

Take care of your lamb.
Take care of animals.

UNIT 7

My Family

Hello, Grandma. This is for you.
This is for me?
Oh, thank you! Thank you!
A nice surprise for me.

[Chorus]
Be good to your family.
All your family.

Hello, Grandpa. This is for you.
A hug for me?
Oh, thank you! Thank you!
A nice, big hug for me.

[Chorus]

UNIT 9

My Clothes

I have a jacket.
Look at my jacket.
My jacket is yellow.

Put on your jacket,
your yellow jacket.
Dress yourself today.

I have two shoes.
Look at my shoes.
My shoes are white.

Put on your shoes,
your white shoes.
Dress yourself today.

UNIT 10

Outside

[Chorus]
Come outside.
Explore outside.
Explore outside with me!

Look at the birds.
How many birds?
Three birds—one, two, three.

[Chorus]

Look at the flowers.
How many flowers?
Three flowers—one, two, three.

Aa
alligator

Bb
beaver

Cc
camel

Dd
duck

Ii
iguana

Jj
jaguar

Kk
kangaroo

Ll
lion

Qq
quail

Rr
reindeer

Ss
seal

Tt
tiger

Uu
umbrellabird

Ee
elephant

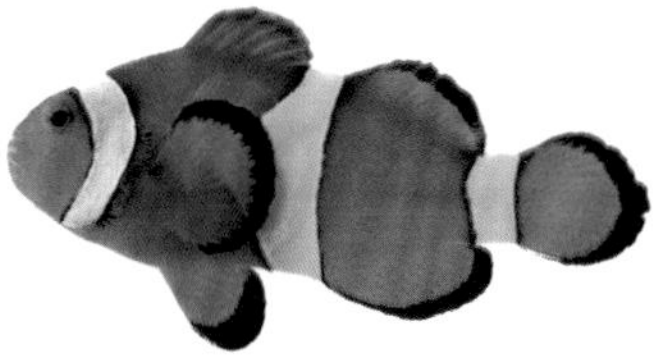

Ff
fish

Gg
gorilla

Hh
hippo

Mm
monkey

Nn
numbat

Oo
octopus

Pp
panda

Vv
vulture

Ww
wolf

Xx
fo**x**

Yy
yak

Zz
zebra

CREDITS

PHOTOS: 2 (t) © Jan Zammit; (mt) Courtesy of Frank DeJongh/UNICEF; (m) joey333/iStock/Getty Images; (mb) Xinhua News Agency/Getty Images; (b) Look/Alamy Stock Photo; **3** (t) © Inge Johnsson; (mt) © John Stanmeyer; (m) © Charlie Hamilton James/National Geographic Image Collection; (mb) Otographer/Pilar Olivares/Reuters; (b) © Courtesy of Ajar Setiadi; **4** Courtesy of UNICEF/UNI138867/Haque; **5** © Jan Zammit; **6** (tl) Kativ/E+/Getty Images; (tr) David Hanson/Aurora Photos; (bl) paultarasenko/Shutterstock.com; (bm) Tetra Images, LLC/Alamy Stock Photo; (br) AustinandAugust/Shutterstock.com; (background) praetorianphoto/iStock/Getty Images; **8** AT Photography/Moment/Getty Images; **9** (t) Joel Sartore/National Geographic Image Collection; (b) reptiles4all/Shutterstock.com; **10** Design Pics Inc/Alamy Stock Photo; (project) © 2021 Cengage; **11** Courtesy of Frank DeJongh/UNICEF; **12** (tl) ZouZou/Shutterstock.com; (tm) iprachenko/Shutterstock.com; (tr) Mega Pixel/Shutterstock.com; (m) John Kasawa/Shutterstock.com; (b) Juris Kraulis/Alamy Stock Photo; (background) Keith Levit/Perspectives/Getty Images; **13** (tl) tavizta/Shutterstock.com; (tm) chalrumpon onnongwa/Shutterstock.com; (tr) daizuoxin/Shutterstock.com; (bl) Natalya Erofeeva/Shutterstock.com; (br) AlexKrul/Shutterstock.com; (background) PowerUp/Shutterstock.com; **14** © Annie Griffiths; (inset) Westend61/Getty Images; **15** (t) Sergiy Tryapitsyn/Alamy Stock Photo; (m) Brian A Jackson/Shutterstock.com; (b) recebin/Shutterstock.com; **16** (t) Xinhua/eyevine/Redux; (b) Vano Shlamov/AFP/Getty Images; (project) © 2021 Cengage; **17** joey333/iStock/Getty Images; **18** Mark Mawson/Stone/Getty Images; **19** (all) irin-k/Shutterstock.com; **20** © Children at Risk Foundation; **21** (t) Joel Sartore/National Geographic Image Collection; (b) Andre Klopper/Shutterstock.com; **22** SasPartout/Shutterstock.com; (project) © 2021 Cengage; **23** Xinhua News Agency/Getty Images; **24** (tl) Sintez/iStock/Getty Images; (tr) Dorling Kindersley ltd/Alamy Stock Photo; (ml) CykOtie/Shutterstock.com; (mr) taweesak thiprod/Shutterstock.com; (b) kyoshino/iStock/Getty Images; (background) Celia Peterson/Getty Images; **26** (l) AfriPics.com/Alamy Stock Photo; (r) John Warburton-Lee Photography/Alamy Stock Photo; **27** (t) Twin Design/Shutterstock.com; (m) Chayapon Bootboonneam/EyeEm/Getty Images; (r) Mega Pixel/Shutterstock.com; **28** Nikada/iStock Unreleased/Getty Images; (project) © 2021 Cengage; (l) Layland Masuda/Moment/Getty Images; (ml) Pongnaret Palamon/Shutterstock.com; (mr) paulaphoto/Shutterstock.com; (r) FotoAndalucia/Shutterstock.com; **29** Look/Alamy Stock Photo; **30** Alison Crane Photography/Moment/Getty Images; **31** (tl) Westend61 GmbH/Alamy Stock Photo; (tml) Dave King/Dorling Kindersley/Getty Images; (tmr) Werli Francois/Alamy Stock Photo; (tr) Karen Anderson/Moment Open/Getty Images; (bl) Apichet Chakreeyarut/Alamy Stock Photo; (bml) ViewStock/Getty Images; (bmr) sarahwolfephotography/Moment/Getty Images; (br) Maisie Paterson/Tetra images/Getty Images; (background) natrot/Shutterstock.com; **32** Philipp Engelhorn/laif/Redux; **33** (t) Joel Sartore/National Geographic Photo Ark/National Geographic Image Collection; (b) Rosa Jay/Shutterstock.com; **34** Larry Dale Gordon/The Image Bank/Getty Images; (project) © 2021 Cengage; **35** © Inge Johnsson; **36** (t) pidjoe/istock/Getty Images; (ml) Cheers Group/Shutterstock.com; (mm) Sergey Ivanychev/EyeEm/Getty Images; (mr) Tarasyuk Igor/Shutterstock.com; (b) Jiri Hera/Shutterstock.com; (background) Johanna Parkin/Photolibrary/Getty Images; **37** (tl) gu min/Shutterstock.com; (tm) sta/Shutterstock.com; (tr) Suzanne Tucker/Shutterstock.com; (bl) Tania Bertoni/Shutterstock.com; (bm) gowithstock/Shutterstock.com; (br) abimages/Shutterstock.com; (background) weedezign/Shutterstock.com; **38** brytta/iStock/Getty Images; **39** (tl) Cheers Group/Shutterstock.com; (tr) Sergey Ivanychev/EyeEm/Getty Images; (m) Anna Kucherova/Shutterstock.com; (b) Peter Dazeley/Photographer's Choice/Getty Images; **40** (tl) hacohob/Shutterstock.com; (tm) Valentina Razumova/Shutterstock.com; (tm/background) kzww/Shutterstock.com; (tr) Lumikk555/iStock/Getty Images; (bl) Robert Schneider/Alamy Stock photo; (br) Ixefra/Moment/Getty Images; (project) © 2021 Cengage; **41** © John Stanmeyer; **42** subodhsathe/iStock/Getty Images; **44** (t) Halfpoint/iStock/Getty Images; (b) Jose Luis Pelaez Inc/DigitalVision/Getty Images; **45** (t, b) Joel Sartore/National Geographic Image Collection; **46** (t) David Lazar/Moment Select/Getty Images; (b) Anup Shah/Nature Picture Library; (project) © 2021 Cengage; imageBROKER/Alamy Stock Photo; **47** © Charlie Hamilton James/National Geographic Image Collection; **48** (l) pirita/Shutterstock.com; (ml) yuris/Shutterstock.com; (m) Matteo Fagiolino/Moment/Getty Images; (mr) MiaQu/Shutterstock.com; (r) IonelV/Shutterstock.com; (background) John Eveson/Minden Pictures; **49** (tl. tmlb) © Virginia Collins/EyeEm/Getty Images; (tmlt) © Sherjaca/Shutterstock.com; (tmr, trb) © Nicole Mulstay/Shutterstock.com; (trt) © Maika 777/Moment/Getty Images; (bl, brb) © chaoss/Shutterstock.com; (brt) © Skumer/Shutterstock.com; (background) © goory/Shutterstock.com; **50** (l) Belinda Dimarzio-Bryan/EyeEm/Getty Images; (r) Cavan Images/Cavan/Getty Images; **51** (tl) Kuznetsov Alexey/Shutterstock.com; (tr) Valentina_S/Shutterstock.com; (m) prochasson frederic/Shutterstock.com; (b) Chris Winsor/Moment/Getty Images; **52** (tl) Alfribeiro/iStock/Getty Images; (tr) PaulGrecaud/iStock/Getty Images; (b) Walter Bibikow/age fotostock/Robert Harding; (project) © 2021 Cengage; **53** Otographer/Pilar Olivares/Reuters; **54** (t) Iuliia Syrotina/Shutterstock.com; (ml) SakisPagonas/Shutterstock.com; (mr) New Africa/Shutterstock.com; (b) PhotoAlto/Laurence Mouton/PhotoAlto Agency RF Collections/Getty Images; (background) Menno Boermans/Cavan/Alamy Stock Photo; **55** (l) baona/iStock/Getty Images; (m) Watthano/Shutterstock.com; (r) Hogan Imaging/Shutterstock.com; (background) Alexlukin/Shutterstock.com; **56** (l) Westend61/Getty Images; (r) Dorling Kindersley/Getty Images; **57** (t) Joel Sartore/National Geographic Image Collection; (b) Ignacio Yufera/Biosphoto/Alamy Stock Photo; **58** (tl) berna namoglu/Shutterstock.com; (tr) Norbert Scanella/Robert Harding; (bl) elina nova/Shutterstock.com; (br) Halfpoint/iStock/Getty Images; (project) © Cengage; **59** Courtesy of Ajar Setiadi; **60** (l) rsooll/Shutterstock.com; (ml) KasperczakBohdan/Shutterstock.com; (mr) Brian Jannsen/Alamy Stock Photo; (r) Pavaphon Supanantananont/Shutterstock.com; (background) TomasSereda/iStock/Getty Images; **62** (t) Bence Mate/Nature Picture Library; (b) draasipos0323/iStock/Getty Images; **63** (tl) Fotofermer/Shutterstock.com; (tr) Barbol/Shutterstock.com; (m) Olhastock/Shutterstock.com; (b) Super Prin/Shutterstock.com; **64** (tl) robertharding/Image Bank Film/Getty Images; (tm) Discovod/Getty Images; (tr) National Geographic Image Collection; (b) Multi-bits/Image Bank Film/Getty Images; (project) © 2021 Cengage; **65** (l) AT Photography/Moment/Getty Images; (r) Annie Griffiths/NGL Life as Lived; **66** (l) © Children at Risk Foundation; (r) John Warburton-Lee Photography/Alamy Stock Photo; **67** (l) Philipp Engelhorn/laif/Redux; (r) brytta/iStock/Getty Images; **68** (l) Jose Luis Pelaez Inc/DigitalVision/Getty Images; (r) Belinda Dimarzio-Bryan/EyeEm/Getty Images; **69** (l) Westend61/Getty Images; (r) Bence Mate/Nature Picture Library; **70** (tl, bmr, br) Joel Sartore/National Geographic Image Collection; (tml, tmr, tr, ml, mml, mmr, mr, bl, bml, bm) Joel Sartore/National Geographic Photo Ark/National Geographic Image Collection; **71** (tl, mr, bml) Joel Sartore/National Geographic Image Collection; (tml, tmr, tr, ml, mml, mr, bl, bm, bmr, br) Joel Sartore/National Geographic Photo Ark/National Geographic Image Collection; **Back Cover** Joel Sartore/National Geographic Image Collection.

ILLUSTRATIONS: All mascot artwork created by Fabiana Faiallo; **7, 25, 61** Jill Dubin/Painted Words, Claire Easton; **8, 14, 20, 26, 32, 38, 43, 44, 50, 56, 62** Fabiana Faiallo; **19** Mary Rojas/Maggie Beyer Sprinzeles.